Pebble® Plus

# Animal Communication

by Abbie Dunne

C016392269

raintree
a Capstone company — publishers for children

Raintree is an imprint of Capstone Global Library Limited, a company incorporated in England and Wales having its registered office at 264 Banbury Road, Oxford, OX2 7DY – Registered company number: 6695582

www.raintree.co.uk
myorders@raintree.co.uk

Edited by Linda Staniford
Designed by Bobbie Nuytten
Picture research by Jo Miller
Production by Tori Abraham

ISBN 978-1-474-72252-0  (hardback)
20  19  18  17  16
10 9 8 7 6 5 4 3 2 1

ISBN 978-1-474-72276-6  (paperback)
21  20  19  18  17
10 9 8 7 6 5 4 3 2 1

**British Library Cataloguing in Publication Data**
A full catalogue record for this book is available from the British Library.

**Acknowledgements**
We would like to thank the following for permission to reproduce photographs: Minden Pictures: Kim Taylor, 5; Science Source: E. R. Degginger, 19; Shutterstock: Chones, 20, Eric Gevaert, 11, MarcusVDT, 21, Olga Visavi, 17, Paul Reeves Photography, 1, 7, Rejja, 13, Rob Hainer, cover, steve estvanik, 15; Thinkstock: Jupiterimages/PHOTOS.com, 9

Design Elements
Shutterstock: Alena P

Printed and bound in China.

# Contents

# How do animals communicate?

Animals can't talk.

But they do communicate.

Whales sing underwater.

Bees dance to tell other bees

where to find food.

# Sound

Birds sing to send messages to other birds. One song may mean, "Come and build a nest with me." Another song may signal danger.

# Smell

Smell tells animals many things. It tells them whether to come or go. A moth's scent attracts other moths. A skunk's stinky spray says, "Stay away!"

# Body language

Animals use their bodies
to communicate, too.
Nervous chimpanzees show
their teeth. Gorillas frown
when they are worried.

Sometimes dogs wag their tails
to say they are happy. When dogs
want to play, they lower their
upper bodies to the ground.

# Touch

A touch can say many things. Elephants show love by touching trunks. Cats rub their owner's leg when they want attention.

# Colours and lights

Octopuses communicate

by changing their skin colour.

The colours are signals

to other octopuses.

Some animals communicate
with light. Fireflies glow
in the darkness. The flashes
of light send messages
to other fireflies.

# Activity

How do honeybees tell each other where to find nectar? Find out!

## What you need

- group of friends or family
- packets of sugar or sugar cubes
- floor space

## What you do

1. Name one person the scout bee. Everyone else is a worker bee.

2. Ask everyone except the scout bee to leave the room. Ask the scout bee to hide the sugar.

3. Ask the scout bee to make up a dance. The dance should tell the worker bees where to find the sugar.

4. Ask everyone to come back into the room. Then ask the scout bee to perform the dance.

5. Ask the worker bees to find the sugar. Did any bees find it?

6. Choose a new scout bee and repeat steps 2–5.

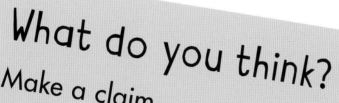

## What do you think?

Make a claim.

A claim is something you believe to be true.

How do honeybees tell other bees where to find food?

# Glossary

**attention**  playing, talking, and being with someone
or something

**attract**  get the attention of someone
or something

**communicate**  share information, thoughts,
or feelings

**message**  facts, ideas or feelings sent to someone
or something

**nervous**  uneasy or worried

**scent**  smell

**signal**  message between our brains and
our senses

**underwater**  under the surface of the water

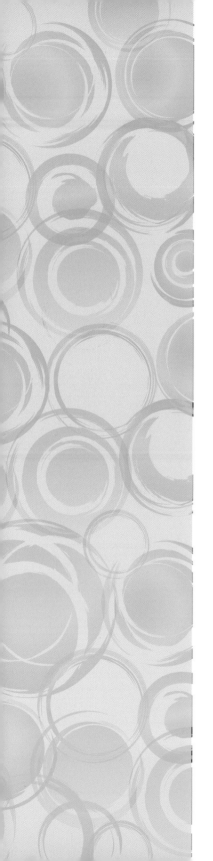

# Find out more

## Books

*Amazing Animal Communicators* (Animal Superpowers), John Townsend (Raintree, 2013)

*Monkeys* (Animals are Amazing), Valerie Bodden (Franklin Watts, 2012)

*Whales* (Animals are Amazing), Kate Riggs (Franklin Watts, 2012)

## Websites

**www.bbc.co.uk/nature/adaptations/ Hearing_%28sense%29**

Hear some of the sounds animals make to communicate with each other at this site.

**kids.britannica.com/comptons/article-9272879/animal-communication]**

Find out more about how animals communicate here.

**ypte.org.uk/factsheets/communication-in-animals/scent**

The Young People's Trust for the Environment website explains about animal communication.

# Comprehension questions

1. Explain what communication means.

2. List three ways in which animals communicate.

3. A skunk's spray smells terrible. What do you think this communicates to other animals?

4. Why do you think animals that live in dark places use lights to communicate with each other?

# Index